Real Boy

Finn A. Evans & Ramonah N.J. Gibson

The Script:

After moving to yet another new school and unexpectedly making friends with a hypermasculine trans ally, a gender-questioning teenager must fight back against bullies, friends, and his mother to finally embrace his identity as a trans boy. Will he succeed or succumb to his people-pleasing ways?

The Authors:

Finn A. Evans is an American-born, Bulgarian-raised writer and director who holds both a BA in Media Studies and an MA in Theatre Directing from the University of East Anglia. His focus is on creating stories - through film, radio drama, and the stage - which explore misrepresented demographics and rarely discussed topics.

Evident in both his international debut film 'Glow' in 2021 (on turbulent mental health) to directing 2022's 'Real Boy' (representing the rarely appreciated reality to being transgender), is his belief that amazing things are done by people opening their hearts and uniting in a common goal.

Ramonah N.J. Gibson is a Liberian & American scriptwriter, and holds a MA in Creative Writing: Scriptwriting from the University of East Anglia. Growing up a third-culture kid living her childhood predominantly abroad, her main connection to Western culture was through entertainment. This is where her understanding of entertainment's power stems from. Through her screenwriting, Ramonah works to close the gap between the reality of everyday minority lives and their portrayal on screens and stages. In this way she hopes to normalize and raise awareness for their experiences.

Real Boy

by

Finn A. Evans & Ramonah N.J. Gibson

Chudatsi Publishing

1st Edition, June 2023

ISBN 978-1-7394248-0-0

Cover Art by Isel Porta
Edited by Amie M Marie

Chudatsi Publishing

On the 22nd of October 2022, *Real Boy* was first performed to an audience at the University of East Anglia Drama Studio, Norwich with the following cast

REAL BOY	Jesse Smith
YOUNG REAL BOY	Sam Nuttal
MOTHER	Kira Moss
JAIME	Elena Hrant
FIGARO	Will Mullet
TRUMAN	Nabil Dozoum
DR. OLDRIK & NURSE	Victoria Coleman
HEAD BULLY	Will Stephenson
BULLY 1	Gabriel Tiller
BULLY 2	Elliott Lecointe

Special thanks to the debut crew

Danail Vidinsky, Composer. Tao (Bogi) Burin, Dance and Movement Choreographer. Sabrina Poole, Stage Fight Coordinator. Sam Rook, Costume Designer. Tori Simpson, Light and Sound Technician. Lindsay Williams, Social Media. Amie M Marie, PR. Henry Webb, Photographer. Isel Porta, Poster Designer. Cinematographers: Joshua Whittington, Samuel Franks, Drew Burgess

---

Note: Jaime is initially costumed as a green creature and sheds layers during the show into a more approachable appearance. Dr. Oldrik and Nurse must be played by the same performer.

It is strongly advised that the character of Real Boy is always performed by a transgender actor, whenever this would **not endanger** the cast and crew through outing or backlash.

Introduction to Real Boy

Written by a trans-man and a black woman, Real Boy is a love letter to queer and trans youth and their loved ones. It's a story about navigating a world that does not accept you and the dangers of not accepting and loving yourself.

We wrote this story knowing it would reflect exact scenarios for some, while hoping it would shed enough light to change the future path of others. We wrote this story to heal and comfort queer and trans youth and to show cis folk the multiple factors that contribute to trans lives.

Many people believe they've never met a trans person and therefore are uncertain as to why their rights are important. We believe that trans rights matter because human rights matter. At the crux of the issue is one simple truth. Trans people are people, and every person has a right to be who they want and love who they love, without discrimination from others. Trans people are under attack daily for a reality they did not choose and can not change, which is why the trans community needs vocal support. We wrote Real Boy to provide that vocal support and invoke inclusive community spaces.

While targeted at trans and queer youth, Real Boy contains a universal message about the consequences of people-pleasing and losing yourself in the desires of others. People-pleasing doesn't discriminate based on gender. While seen as a common trait, we felt it important to highlight and explore its consequences in this play.

Real Boy is not meant to shame or convince people of anything. We are not imposing ideas; instead, we've tried to present different points of view and encourage and hope that our audience uses their experience of the play to think critically. Entertainment is the unguarded door to sharing human experiences. Through entertainment, we are more open to other perspectives. After all, characters and storylines are fictional. Entertainment creates a non-judgmental space for people to confront their ideas about people different from them.

Theatre does this in a most impactful way. Unlike television or film with actors on a two-dimensional platform having said words a long time ago, theatre gives an immediate, three-dimensional immersive experience.

Theatre is direct and inescapable. While we hope to one day adapt Real Boy to the screen and reach a wider audience, its original iteration is Theatre. Because only in theatre can the immersive, immediate experience take place. Only in theatre can actors react to an audience and vice versa. This accelerates emotion and understanding that other forms of entertainment can not. For such an important topic and the critical thinking we hope to inspire, we felt that connection to the audience was most important when selecting the medium of our story.

Our greatest wish is for you, the reader/audience, to enjoy and learn something, anything, from our story. Whether you learn about yourself or others, we hope you take away the tools needed to think about the difficult topics brought up in our play.

Sincerely,

Finn A. Evans & Ramonah N.J. Gibson

Scene 1

Darkness. We hear jumbled music, commercials, cartoons. Then, with clarity: When You Wish Upon A Star by Cliff Edwards. Lights snap on to a dim state.

This is Home. YOUNG REAL BOY sits with his back to the audience, lit by the colourful glow of a television. MOTHER stands at the periphery, busying herself. The television gives one last burst of sound before -

TELEVISION: I want to be a real boy!

- the television turns off.

Lights brighten.

The audience can now see what YOUNG REAL BOY is wearing: a skirt, baseball hat, and t-shirt.

YOUNG REAL BOY leaps upright, full of joy. MOTHER removes his hat to reveal two long ponytails.

MOTHER   You're so pretty, darling.

They sit together. The TV flickers back on. Stage lights dim. Only the TV and its glow is visible. We hear it jutter and loop as Pinocchio discovers that he's a real boy again and again. Blackout.

Scene 2

REAL BOY is dressed in a pair of pants, loafers, and a nice top. His style is androgynous but still safe for society. MOTHER rushes around, formally and femininely dressed.

MOTHER Wait! Before we leave-

MOTHER presents a perfume bottle and spritzes herself. She attempts to spritz REAL BOY. He dodges.

REAL BOY I told you I don't like that one.

MOTHER Well it's the only one of my bottles I can find.

REAL BOY I don't need perfume!

MOTHER We're going to your cousin's wedding. Do you want to smell at your cousin's wedding?

REAL BOY I don't smell bad. I showered.

MOTHER Well, you don't smell good.

REAL BOY I don't smell. Isn't that good enough?

MOTHER   No. Why do you fight me on every little thing? It's just perfume. It won't kill you. I only want you to be your best when you walk out the door. That's all. A young lady should always smell good.

REAL BOY I don't like the perfume. It's a small thing. Please, we're almost late anyway.

It appears that MOTHER concedes defeat. She offers a hug. REAL BOY embraces MOTHER. As they hug, MOTHER sprays his hair and back with the perfume.

MOTHER   See? It really isn't that bad.

REAL BOY The only reason I'm going is because I love my cousin. Not for you.

MOTHER   Of course you love her. Wish you would be more like her.

REAL BOY walks out.

Scene 3

We're in a child's bedroom. YOUNG REAL BOY sleeps. There's a blue light shining from above, sinking YOUNG REAL BOY into a pool of electric-dark-blue shadows. The music is uncomfortable, synthetic, with throat singing that builds.

JAIME enters, freakily, with buglike green clothing. Moving in a slow-fast animal fashion, JAIME examines the room, the audience, and looms over YOUNG REAL BOY. It's a terrifying sight to wake up to.

YOUNG REAL BOY opens his eyes, panics, struggles to escape the tight and heavy bedding.

JAIME covers YOUNG REAL BOY's mouth. YOUNG REAL BOY mumbles and screams.

MOTHER enters.

JAIME scrambles to hide, vanishing from MOTHER's possible sight. MOTHER makes a phone call.

MOTHER   Hi. Is this Star Children's Psychology? Yes. I'd like to make an appointment for my daughter with a therapist first thing-

Scene 4

A classroom, students facing the audience. REAL BOY has done well. HEAD BULLY, BULLY 1, and BULLY 2 are scornful.

TEACHER   You should all take note of Real Boy's extraordinary performance.

The three BULLIES taunt in whispers.

ALL BULLIES   Puppet, puppet on strings, we're gonna cut off your wings. Puppet, puppet on strings, we're gonna cut off your wings.

The three BULLIES move in closer, pulling on rope and affecting REAL BOY's actions. The BULLIES are louder now.

ALL BULLIES   Come on, Real Boy! Give us the answers like a good little puppet!

REAL BOY is physically manipulated into nodding. His arm snaps out, handing over notes. The BULLIES continue to manipulate REAL BOY. What we see is cruel.

REAL BOY lands on the floor. His shoelaces are tied. The BULLIES loom. HEAD BULLY puts a shoe on REAL BOY's head, keeping him down.

BULLY 1   You love being a teacher's pet, don't you, bootlicker?

ALL BULLIES   Bootlicker! Bootlicker! Bootlicker!

HEAD BULLY   Can't be too harsh. It's not her fault. She needs to be a bootlicker. She's a freak. Doesn't even know how to be a girl. No one wants to be friends with... The joke is, the teachers are being paid extra to be her friend.

They laugh. REAL BOY tries and fails to stop this.

HEAD BULLY   Give us what we want and you won't have to lick my shoe. Tick-tock, it's up to you, bootlicker!

ALL BULLIES   Tick-tock around the clock, you are turning into a wooden stock!

They chant, taunt, and physically move REAL BOY. First upright from on the floor, then arms out, wrists bent and head hung. He's halfway between a lifeless marionette and a person trapped in a wooden stock.

ALL BULLIES   Tick-tock around the clock, you're turning into a wooden stock! Tick-tock around the clock, you're turning into a wooden stock!

TRUMAN enters. His sudden presence startles us.

TRUMAN   What's happening here? (*Pause*) I asked, what's going on?

HEAD BULLY lands one last hit on REAL BOY.

TRUMAN   Let him go.

HEAD BULLY   Or what?

TRUMAN   Or I will beat you up. Unlike him, I'm no bootlicker - but I can make you one!

TRUMAN unhooks a decorative trouser chain and wraps it around his knuckles. He's serious.

TRUMAN   So, which is it?

We see hesitation. The HEAD BULLY makes a gesture. REAL BOY is released.

HEAD BULLY   You'll regret this.

TRUMAN   I'm sure I will. Now get lost.

TRUMAN offers a hand to REAL BOY.

TRUMAN   The first beatings are always the hardest. Up!

Scene 5

A clean, bright therapist's office. It's claustrophobic. The clock ticks a little too fast. We hear the dry scribbling of pen on paper.

DR. OLDRIK   Hello, dear. How are you today?

YOUNG REAL BOY is unmoved.

DR. OLDRIK   Do you know why you're here?

JAIME sits next to YOUNG REAL BOY. She's invisible to DR. OLDRIK.

DR. OLDRIK   Is there something wrong with the couch, dear?

YOUNG BOY   No, not really.

DR. OLDRIK   You've told your parents that you don't like the girl's uniform and prefer the boy's one. Is that true?

YOUNG REAL BOY looks towards JAIME. JAIME slowly shakes their head, telling REAL BOY to lie.

YOUNG BOY   Is that why I am here?

DR. OLDRIK   No. But the other children are not nice to you when you wear the boy uniform. Correct? You're here so that I can help you find solutions to your problems. All of them. From the night terrors to the bullying which I suspect are connected.

YOUNG BOY   I find wearing skirts in winter cold, don't you?

JAIME nods. DR OLDRIK is appeased.

DR. OLDRIK   You're very smart! I can't argue with such a good point. (*under her breath*) Very smart, indeed.

YOUNG BOY   Is that bad? You're writing.

DR. OLDRIK   Being very smart is never bad. You're a smart little girl and I am here to make sure you're a happy smart little girl. Sometimes the world punishes smart people for being smart but I will never punish you for being who you are. I am just writing down how smart you are. So that I never forget. I am your friend.

Ok? (*Beat*) Now, our session is over but please send your mother in on the way out. I need to speak to her.

YOUNG REAL BOY exits. MOTHER enters, flustered and afraid. The invisible JAIME watches.

MOTHER   Is she going to be ok? I just want her to be ok. Did I do something wrong?

Scene 6

REAL BOY is at home, setting up a video game on the TV. He's waiting for his friend to arrive.

FIGARO   Hey hey hey!

REAL BOY   Figaro!

A special handshake.

FIGARO   Glad to see you haven't forgotten it since moving to the new school.

REAL BOY   Never!

They sit in front of the TV and play.

FIGARO   So. How is it?

REAL BOY   Eh, it's a school. Children go in and are tortured for eight hours. Then they're released.

FIGARO   Ok... Is your torture less?

REAL BOY   You know bullies follow me everywhere I go. But I've made a new friend that defended me. I guess he's my new school's Figaro.

FIGARO   I'm irreplaceable baby!

REAL BOY   Duh! You can't replace ten years of world-class protection with one save.

FIGARO   So all I am is muscle to you?

REAL BOY   No! You're also the guy I've been beating in video games for ten years!

REAL BOY reaches across to mess with FIGARO's controller, giving himself a lead in the game.

FIGARO   No! Cheater!

REAL BOY   Life isn't fair!

FIGARO   I know. I'm happy you've found a new friend. I wish you didn't have to change schools.

REAL BOY   Me too. But it's fine. Time for us to figure out who we are not as a duo.

FIGARO   Apparently, we're not that different even apart.

FIGARO goes to disrupt REAL BOY's controller. REAL BOY yelps playfully.

Scene 7

At school, between classes. REAL BOY's shoelaces dangle untied. TRUMAN enters and barely bumps into REAL BOY, who stumbles and catches himself.

TRUMAN You always risking your balance like that? No one told you how to tie these correctly? You need to double knot them.

TRUMAN tuts before kneeling down. He ties REAL BOY's shoelace on one shoe.

TRUMAN See? Better. Right? Now, try with your other shoe, come on!

REAL BOY hurries to kneel, ties his other shoe's laces.

TRUMAN Good. This is your first step to not being a bootlicker. People won't make you trip. Wanna hang for lunch?

REAL BOY Umhm.

TRUMAN Listen, you did so well on the test last time -

REAL BOY   I'm not going to give you answers.

TRUMAN   I'm not asking for that. Will you tutor me? Sort of an exchange.

REAL BOY   Yeah, for what?

TRUMAN   You teach me. I teach you. How to...do things... So that you don't have trouble with bullies like that anymore.

REAL BOY   Like Karate?

TRUMAN   Yeah. But mental Karate. Like Confucius, Art of War stuff. I didn't have to actually fight anyone when I saved you did I? I'll teach you.

REAL BOY   Why? Wouldn't me giving you the answers be easier?

TRUMAN   Do you want to give me the answers? Be honest.

REAL BOY   No.

TRUMAN   Let's start. I'm going to eat this lunch and after, I gotta go to the bathroom.

REAL BOY   Ok?

TRUMAN   You going to come with me?

REAL BOY   Yeah?

TRUMAN   Good.

Both boys open their lunches.

REAL BOY   Why help me?

TRUMAN   I told you why.

REAL BOY   It's not the real reason.

TRUMAN   ... You get Ham & Cheese too?

REAL BOY   Yeah, on wheat.

TRUMAN   Your Mama make that sandwich?

REAL BOY   Yeah. She did. Yours too, huh?

TRUMAN   No.

REAL BOY   Oh.

TRUMAN   I'm helping you because I know what it's like. To be alien. To be odd. A freak. Not accepted and not understood. Even by the people who should.

Scene 8

The therapist's office. It's still claustrophobic. The clock ticks a little too fast.

DR. OLDRIK   So, night terrors, huh? Could you tell me more about that green creature you mentioned?

YOUNG BOY   It feels hard to breath when it's there. It stands over me. It dances. Mama can't see it. Even when Mama comes into the room at night.

DR. OLDRIK   Does it attack Mama?

YOUNG BOY   No. It always leaves when Mama comes in.

DR. OLDRIK   Ok. Dear, do you think maybe it leaves because Mama is a girl?

YOUNG BOY   No. I think it leaves because it's scared of Mama.

DR. OLDRIK   I think you're right. I think that it knows that Mama knows it's trying to confuse you.

YOUNG BOY   Why?

DR. OLDRIK   Dear, these night terrors and being bullied at school are all connected. And why are you being bullied?

YOUNG BOY   I don't know.

DR. OLDRIK   Oh, you're a smart little girl. You know.

There is a long pause.

YOUNG BOY   Because I'm different? Because I'm smart. You said people punish smart people.

DR. OLDRIK   I did say that. But I think that the reason why they're punishing you are your clothes. And some of the things you say. Now I know you wear the boys' clothes because it's cold. But being cold is a small sacrifice to make for no more bullying, hmm? And no more bullying would probably lessen the night terrors.

YOUNG BOY   I-

DR. OLDRIK   Your night terrors are scared of Mama. Because she's a girl. You need to start hanging around other girls. At school. Not just Mama. I know Figaro is your friend, and you should keep him. But you need more friends. More normalcy.

YOUNG BOY   But I don't like the things the girls like. I don't want to talk about boys and-

DR. OLDRIK   But you talk about Figaro all the time. You like Figaro.

YOUNG BOY   Yes. But I want to be like Figaro too. Maybe I'm a boy?

DR. OLDRIK   What?

YOUNG BOY   You said it's afraid of girls. But it's not afraid of me. So maybe I'm not a girl?

DR. OLDRIK   You are. You just aren't acting like a girl.

YOUNG BOY   But if you're born a girl why do you have to act like it? To scare creatures away? Shouldn't they just know?

DR. OLDRIK   I-

YOUNG BOY   You're the only one who tells me things. If you don't know then I don't know!

DR. OLDRIK   I do know. I'm sorry. I've just confused you with grown up words. You're so smart sometimes I forget. You are a girl. No matter what. Your night creature must be scared of Mama for some other reason. We'll fix it. We'll fight it. Don't worry. It's not you. Ok?

YOUNG BOY   Ok.

DR. OLDRIK   But dear, do try for me. For your Mama too, ok? I know you get cold, but at least try the skirt. It's spring now, and I would like you to make more friends. Besides me, Mama and Figaro.

Scene 9

REAL BOY's home. It should be comfortable. It isn't.

REAL BOY   Figaro, you would love this guy. We'd all have so much fun.

FIGARO   Yeah? Why's that?

REAL BOY   He's just so... real. Since saving me my first week in school, he's just been chill to hang with. He treats me like a Real Boy.

FIGARO   I do too.

REAL BOY   Well, yeah.

FIGARO   So then...

REAL BOY   Which is why, the three of us could all have so much fun together.

FIGARO   What's he into?

REAL BOY   Like what?

FIGARO	Is he into cars? Video Games? TV? Music? What does he do?
REAL BOY	Honestly, I'm not quite sure yet. We both like Fall Out Boy. Cause I was listening to that and he said it was good.
FIGARO	And that's the only music you know he likes?
REAL BOY	Yes.
FIGARO	You don't find that a bit weird?
REAL BOY	A little. But I'll ask him on Monday, so it's fine.
FIGARO	So, do you guys only talk about his interests then? Seems selfish.
REAL BOY	No. Cause then I'd know more about what he was into.
FIGARO	What do you do together? Do you go to the park and just hangout? Talking?
REAL BOY	Yes.

FIGARO   You don't seem to know much about him. What do you even talk to him about?

REAL BOY   Life.

FIGARO   Life?

REAL BOY   Yeah.

FIGARO laughs.

REAL BOY   What? What's so funny?

FIGARO   You said it so serious. Life.

REAL BOY   That's what we talk about. It's good to talk about it with someone.

FIGARO   Isn't that what we're doing right now? Talking about life. I talk to you about life.

REAL BOY   Yes. Truman and I do it a little different though.

FIGARO   I bet you do.

REAL BOY   Which is why I think we should all hang out together. He's a really chill dude.

FIGARO   Who you barely know anything about. Alright. If you like him I like him. I'm glad he saved you from the bullies. I need to thank him at least for keeping my best friend safe. We should hang. Maybe next weekend?

REAL BOY   Oh, he can't, we've got some other plans together. Weekend after?

FIGARO   That should work. I'm excited.

Scene 10

A grassy park, at dusk. TRUMAN and REAL BOY hang out below the Milky Way: stars twinkle and streetlights are a fuzzy amber.

TRUMAN	The other day you said it feels hard for you to stand your ground. I could see that when we first met. The most important thing is to believe in yourself. You need to believe what you already know. Be confident. When you want to prove your point, talk slower, calmer. Also, this calmness should reflect in the way you walk too. Come on, let me see you walk.

TRUMAN pushes REAL BOY forward, as encouragement. With a moment's consideration, REAL BOY walks in a stiff, wooden way. TRUMAN observes, laughs, then stops him. He fixes REAL BOY's stance.

TRUMAN	Okay, you shouldn't be so stiff. It should come naturally.

They try again. It's not much better.

TRUMAN huffs and demonstrates the way REAL BOY is moving - arms and legs all wrong! - verses the way TRUMAN wants him to move.

REAL BOY tries again, with more confidence, until TRUMAN is happy with the result.

They sit and observe the stars. TRUMAN looks towards REAL BOY. REAL BOY has crossed his legs.

TRUMAN   Not to be a perfectionist but-

TRUMAN slaps REAL BOY's knees apart, having REAL BOY man-spread.

TRUMAN   There we go.

REAL BOY is confused, then laughs. They look up in peaceful silence. TRUMAN pulls out a joint. REAL BOY tries not to stare.

REAL BOY   Do you often do that?

TRUMAN   Do what?

REAL BOY changes the subject.

REAL BOY   This. Star gaze.

TRUMAN	I like to remind myself at the end of it all, there are things bigger than all of this. The world is bigger than you and me. Than school…than home. This helps to see the bigger things, the bigger picture.

TRUMAN motions towards the joint.

REAL BOY	Really?

TRUMAN	You want to try it? It doesn't bite. I promise.

REAL BOY takes a drag. He coughs. TRUMAN laughs. TRUMAN shows him how it's done. REAL BOY attempts again. He succeeds. They sit in silence.

REAL BOY	Yeah…that's nice.

REAL BOY leans towards TRUMAN's shoulder.

REAL BOY	You don't mind, do you?

TRUMAN	Nah, bigger things, remember?

REAL BOY	Bigger things…

Scene 11

Light snaps up, a very bright interior.

MOTHER　　How was your talk time with Dr. Oldrik?

YOUNG BOY　　It was good! She's so nice!

MOTHER　　She is very nice. And she wants to help. She is helping, darling?

YOUNG BOY　　Yes, Mama.

MOTHER　　Good. You know I always want the best for you darling.

YOUNG BOY　　But Mama, why can't you help me?

MOTHER　　You don't like Dr. Oldrik?

YOUNG BOY　　I do, Mama. But you help me with everything!

MOTHER　　I do help you with everything. I love helping you with everything. But this is one thing I can't help you with. No

	matter how much I want to. Hmm? You understand?
YOUNG BOY	I do.
MOTHER	And Dr. Oldrik is helping. She helped you make the new friend?
YOUNG BOY	Figaro! He's nice.
MOTHER	Yes. He's very nice. You'll see, darling. Soon all of this will stop. You won't need Dr. Oldrik's help anymore. And then, after that, one day you won't need my help either.
YOUNG BOY	I don't know Mama.
MOTHER	But I do know.

Scene 12

Gone is REAL BOY's androgynous haircut. It's fully masc. His clothes reflect his latest transition.

MOTHER   Come on, you've got to go.

REAL BOY   I am going. I'm dressed, aren't I? What fight are you trying to pick today? I'm going to be late.

REAL BOY heads towards the door. MOTHER stops REAL BOY just as he reaches the threshold.

MOTHER   Your school called yesterday. You've skipped twice.

REAL BOY   They're not supposed to do that. I get three full days of skips or six partial day. It's only been-

MOTHER   The fact that you know these specifics is not helping your case. Why are you skipping school? And let's not even talk about how much therapy you've been skipping. Dr. Oldrik told me.

REAL BOY	I don't have time for this. I have to go to said school. Sometimes I just need a break. Rest. Time alone.
MOTHER	You get too much time alone. It leads to all these weird decisions. Like these awful homeless looking clothes.
REAL BOY	Ok Mama.
MOTHER	Why can't you be young and happy? Go buy a new skirt, gossip with friends, read nothing magazines just be young and happy.
REAL BOY	This is me being young and happy. My own way.
MOTHER	But you don't want to go to school. The new school that you moved to just so you could bond with other young and happy people. Your therapist says-
REAL BOY	They don't see me as young and happy.
MOTHER	Why not? What's wrong? Are you being bullied again?

REAL BOY   No. I'm not being bullied again. I
              would tell you.

MOTHER   You were starting to hang around
              people again. I thought you even got a
              boyfriend. That Truman boy? I know I
              secretly hoped it was Figaro but any
              boy and I'd be- What's changed? Did
              he break up with you? There are other
              boys. I guess I shouldn't be surprised.
              No boyfriend. What with the hair. Why
              did you do that to your beautiful hair?
              Is this a cry for help? Is the doctor no
              longer helping? You've been going to
              her for so long I just assumed you still-.
              Even so, we used to talk. Why don't we
              talk anymore?

REAL BOY   There are other things in the world to
              worry about besides me. I am going to
              school.

MOTHER   I can't fix it if you won't tell me what
              to fix.

REAL BOY   There is nothing broken Mama. Even if
              there was, I can't talk to you about it

                because...because...you never. (*pause*) You just wouldn't understand. It's a generational thing.

MOTHER Of course.

REAL BOY I am- I can tell you this. Me and Truman and me and Figaro have never nor will ever date. But I am happy. Happier than I've ever been before. You know I love my doctor. She's always listened.

MOTHER Happy people don't have to run away from school.

REAL BOY Maybe running away from school is when I'm happy. Finally free. But it won't happen again. I love you. Mama, don't you ever feel like something is wrong? No one is telling you it's wrong. There is no smoke to signal fire. But you FEEL it.

MOTHER Yes.

REAL BOY What do you do?

MOTHER   I run. Towards it or away from it depending on the situation.

REAL BOY Yes. You do something. Because to not would have you wondering what if I could have stopped it if I just said something, did something. There would be a feeling of guilt and depression if you ignored it.

MOTHER   Do you feel like that about me?

REAL BOY No. Never mind. I don't know. I-I have to go. I'm already late for school.

MOTHER hugs REAL BOY. It's uncomfortably reminiscent of the first scene.

Scene 13

A dance between JAIME and REAL BOY.

At first, REAL BOY is frightened of JAIME and refuses to follow suggested paths or movements. They begin to sync up, finding joy in their fluidity.

REAL BOY is starting to embrace his masculinity, what that means for him. Insect-like JAIME approves.

Scene 14

REAL BOY's space, where the video games and TV and his interests are. MOTHER yells from off-stage.

MOTHER   Figaro, if you need anything else just yell.

FIGARO   Thank you!

FIGARO   Your mom is really not that bad.

REAL BOY   She's nicer to strangers than she is to me.

FIGARO   I'm not a stranger. I'm basically her second child and she's great to me.

REAL BOY   Yeah, but she didn't birth you! And you don't live here and you have actual parents, so it doesn't count. If you were her actual child, you would feel it.

FIGARO   If you say so.

REAL BOY   I'm serious. The other day she chased me with a perfume bottle.

FIGARO   What?

REAL BOY   She chased me with a perfume bottle. And she insulted my hair. All because I've partially skipped two days of school which isn't even the minimum required for them to call your parents. My grades are still fine.

FIGARO   I'm sorry. But she's kinda right.

REAL BOY   You're never on my side. I don't know why I talk to you.

FIGARO   I am on your side. More than you are sometimes. It's good to go to school. Not because your mom wants you to, but because you like learning. She hates your weird haircut but you still got it right?

REAL BOY   YES.

FIGARO   You can wear the hair cut to school right?

REAL BOY   Yes.

FIGARO   See, it's the little wins.

REAL BOY   I guess. She still made me go see my family smelling like that. I can't wait till I get older and she stops.

FIGARO   She'll never stop. You should've seen my mom to my sister at her wedding. Horrible!

FIGARO snickers, remembering.

REAL BOY   Good thing I'm never getting married.

FIGARO   Never?

Scene 15

The park. TRUMAN and REAL BOY hover, not quite in the scenery.

TRUMAN   Come on. Hurry up!

REAL BOY   You really think I'm ready?

REAL BOY wears a baggy t-shirt and pants with a chain. It's VERY masc, and very close to TRUMAN's fashion.

TRUMAN   Oh, yes! For sure. Time to fully transition. You won't ever be the same after this. You need to face these bullies head on. Your world will shift completely. I promise.

The HEAD BULLY and BULLIES 1 & 2 are stood in a loose circle, smoking cigarettes as they move their weight from foot to foot.

TRUMAN   LISTEN UP! You see my friend over here?! You should give him the same treatment that you give me, alright? Whether I'm with him or not, this bullying will stop.

The BULLIES are astonished.

HEAD BULLY   Tell me, Truman, have you got soft or something for that boy-girl over there? You guys doin' it? Hey, I'm not judging, but don't come here, to our space, and bring your tough guy speech about your girlfriend, when you're not even a tough guy yourself.

The bullies close in on TRUMAN and REAL BOY.

TRUMAN   Well, time to teach you lesson one on being a guy. You PUNCH!

TRUMAN punches HEAD BULLY in the face, who spins and falls down. TRUMAN is chuffed.

TRUMAN   Get in here!

Fighting ensues to music. The bullies end up on the floor, groaning in defeat. TRUMAN & REAL BOY face the audience. They bro fist.

REAL BOY   Now who's the bootlicker?

JAIME walks through the devastation. Disappointed, disgusted, clearly distraught—but goes unnoticed by REAL BOY.

Scene 16

The hostile, thin brightness of home, but REAL BOY is confident anyway.

MOTHER	What's this?

REAL BOY's shoulders rise up.

REAL BOY	What's what?

MOTHER	This new look.

REAL BOY	You like it? It's not much different from before but-

MOTHER	Your clothes.

REAL BOY	I know. They're... Cool.

MOTHER	It's something.

REAL BOY	Ok.

A beat.

MOTHER   You always have to do something. You're never happy not embarrassing me.

REAL BOY   It's not about you.

MOTHER   Of course not. It never is. It's always about you. You're so selfish.

REAL BOY   My clothes are about you? You don't hear it?

MOTHER   Of course it is! People see you, they see me! I have gotten you therapy. I have tried everything! All I ask is that you try too! But no! No!

REAL BOY   Mama, I am trying.

MOTHER   This is not trying. This is you- You will never- I can't. Before I say something you can't handle.

REAL BOY   No. I'm never what? I'm never enough for you.

MOTHER   You'll never be normal! And you'll never be loved by anyone else besides me if you keep up this nonsense. Pushing everyone who cares about you away, turning into something that isn't real. That's grotesque.

REAL BOY   I'm grotesque?

MOTHER   You do it to push people away.

REAL BOY   It doesn't push Truman away.

MOTHER   Ever since you started hanging out with that boy he took your identity and erased it. You're not the daughter I know anymore. You're not my daughter.

REAL BOY   I know. I'm your child. Act like it.

MOTHER   Don't you dare! I do everything for you! I care about you and worry about you, every day. I ask you to simply be normal! Can you do that!? No! Act like I have a child? Act like you know what the word gratitude is.

Scene 17

It's REAL BOY's space, he should be feeling safe here. He stares at FIGARO in disbelief.

FIGARO   Will you be my date?

REAL BOY   What?

FIGARO   My date to prom. I need to bring someone.

REAL BOY   Aren't those usually for people who are in a relationship?

FIGARO   Yes, but not all the time. You can bring friends. And everyone there will have someone except me.

REAL BOY   I don't know if your friends will want me in their pictures.

FIGARO   Everyone knows you.

REAL BOY   I don't think this is a great idea.

FIGARO   Please, just think about it. I don't want to be alone.

REAL BOY   But you know so many other people you can take. I don't believe in prom. You like it, remember? "It's free food, good cake, alcohol if you know how to sneak it and a good time." Those were your exact words.

FIGARO   Which is why it shouldn't be such a burden to come with.

REAL BOY   I-

FIGARO   It's one night. It might even change your mind about big parties.

REAL BOY   Do you actually need someone to go with? Truly?

FIGARO   Yes.

REAL BOY   Why don't I believe you?

FIGARO   I don't know. It's just one night. I've gone to so many of your family events you didn't want to go alone to.

REAL BOY	Because you were invited. It was at your insistence!
FIGARO	Didn't we have fun?
REAL BOY	That was before.
FIGARO	Ok. I understand.

Silence.

REAL BOY	Fine.
FIGARO	Thank you.

Scene 18

We're in a REAL BOY's bedroom. REAL BOY sleeps.

There's a blue light shining from above, again, sinking the blanket-wrapped REAL BOY into a pool of electric-dark-blue shadows. The music is uncomfortable, synthetic, with throat singing that builds and hurts to hear.

REAL BOY is tangled, fretful and deeply unconscious in the bedsheets and can't get out.

JAIME appears, tries to wake REAL BOY gently. Then again, less gently. REAL BOY wakes, panics, gasps: screams.

JAIME flees as REAL BOY falls.

Scene 19

Therapist's office. We can't hear the clock ticking anymore. DR. OLDRIK gives REAL BOY a calculating look, before smiling professionally.

DR. OLDRIK   You seem...changed.

Silence. They stare at each other.

DR. OLDRIK   Please! Sit! You know how things go around here. No need for feeling shy.

DR. OLDRIK   How are you?

REAL BOY   Good. Really good.

DR. OLDRIK   Okay!

She writes that down.

DR. OLDRIK   The night terrors?

REAL BOY   Different.

DR. OLDRIK   Different?

REAL BOY   Not always bad. Not always good. But I think it's getting better.

DR. OLDRIK In what way?

REAL BOY   Well, one of them wasn't even scary. Seemed nice even.

DR. OLDRIK So do you feel like you're overcoming it?

REAL BOY   More that I'm accepting it.

Dr. Oldrik writes.

DR. OLDRIK Ok. So, talk to me. What prompted this new look?

REAL BOY   Well, I took your suggestion from last session. I started thinking about who I wanted to see when I looked in the mirror. This is my Ideal Self. The one you encouraged to show up.

DR. OLDRIK And you're sure this is your Ideal Self?

REAL BOY   Yes.

DR. OLDRIK   How?

REAL BOY just smiles.

DR. OLDRIK   So, how does this new look make you feel?

REAL BOY   I am just more confident and happy like this.

DR. OLDRIK   Hmm.

REAL BOY   Isn't that the goal? Of these sessions.

DR. OLDRIK   These sessions have had many goals over the years. Mitigate the dreams, help build your confidence, help you find friends —

REAL BOY   And you've done all of that. We've done that. The night terrors are lessening. And they aren't always horrible now. I have two friends in Truman and Figaro. I stood up to my bullies.

DR. OLDRIK   Not in an acceptable way.

REAL BOY   Yes but the objective was achieved. I want to thank you Dr. Oldrik. Without you I-

DR. OLDRIK   Are you ending our sessions?

REAL BOY   No. I haven't even thought of that as an option. (Pause.) Of course not. I just wanted to say thank you.

DR. OLDRIK   Good. Because I do think we have more to work on.

REAL BOY   Oh. (Beat) But this is a step in the right direction. It feels right.

DR. OLDRIK   I have also told you on many accounts that the right thing to do is not always the thing that feels the best.

REAL BOY   I know. And I've listened. I stood up to my bullies. It didn't feel great at the time, but I was happy after it was over. But this felt different. I need this.

DR. OLDRIK   What prompts you to see this "need" as your Ideal Self?

REAL BOY   I know how I feel when I walk out the door.

DR. OLDRIK   So, it's a form of becoming part of the world, your surroundings and need of validation from your surroundings? How does Truman dress? I suspect in a similar fashion.

REAL BOY   Yes but-

DR. OLDRIK   He's probably a very handsome boy. And I'm sure very attractive to you.

REAL BOY   That's not-

DR. OLDRIK   The way you dealt with your bullies was Truman's idea as well.

REAL BOY   It was-

DR. OLDRIK   He will not make a good partner. He should have and could have fought them himself instead of bringing you into danger.

REAL BOY   Why should he fight and I not?

DR. OLDRIK   Because you're a girl and he's a boy. A boy you're interested in. Do not let your low sense of self stop you from picking someone who you deserve. Someone who will love and protect you. Not confuse you and force you to-

REAL BOY   He hasn't forced me to do anything.

DR. OLDRIK   Sorry. Encouraged you. Infatuation and wanting to become like the person of your affection isn't unique at your age.

REAL BOY   I don't like Truman like that. He's a friend.

DR. OLDRIK   Just a friend who you talk about constantly, follow like a puppy dog, and incessantly mirror? We've talked about this, many times. What do you think is behind your night terrors?

Silence.

DR. OLDRIK   I suspect your actions against your body and lack of acceptance of reality are the cause. I am here to help and have been doing this long enough now

but I don't think we can achieve any progress if your actions go against my therapy. Role playing a boy and skipping classes won't help with your night terrors. You came years ago for professional help. And I have helped. We've become more than patient and doctor. We've become friends. Let me do my job. Let me help you, friend. We've got to learn where behavior comes from, so we can cut it out, and then we can no longer be labeled that way. Understand? You need to cut this label out of your system. This is my last desperate ask. As a friend.

REAL BOY   Truman says it's ok. As a friend. He likes my look. I like feeling comfortable. He says the world is changing and we're too young to be unhappy.

DR. OLDRIK   Warm and fuzzy feelings all the time are for fairy tales. We work with professional practice and real biology here. Don't fall for your friend's traps. Don't get confused. This extremely

> modernized thinking, ironically,
> prevents people from thinking at all.

A substantial silence.

REAL BOY   I'm thinking.

DR. OLDRIK   Yes.

REAL BOY   About the question you asked at the beginning of this session. Eight years has been a long time. I have changed so much. You haven't.

DR. OLDRIK   I have always tried to be a reliable source of refuge for you. I'm glad I've succeeded.

They stare.

REAL BOY whispers.

REAL BOY   You have tried.

Scene 20

The park. HEAD BULLY walks opposite REAL BOY, who is rightfully suspicious.

REAL BOY   What?

HEAD BULLY   Hey! I'm not testing you anymore. We all get it. You're a badass.

REAL BOY   Yeah?

HEAD BULLY   Yeah. Look. I just wanted to know if you wanted a smoke. That's all. It's something only for the guys.

REAL BOY   Yeah. I've seen you all smoking together.

HEAD BULLY   Well, if you want something stronger I've got that too.

HEAD BULLY shows off a small plastic baggy: there's something in there.

REAL BOY   I'm not into that.

HEAD BULLY   Fine. Not everyone can handle the stronger stuff.

HEAD BULLY puts it away.

HEAD BULLY   Now, do you want to smoke with the boys or not?

REAL BOY   I do.

HEAD BULLY   Good. Then this is your audition. Special one just for you.

HEAD BULLY gifts REAL BOY an unlit joint. REAL BOY slowly takes a hit, then offers one to HEAD BULLY. He refuses. REAL BOY closes his eyes. HEAD BULLY exits.

Scene 21

The park again, magical with twinkling dawn lights. REAL BOY gets up. JAIME sits, calmly staring at him, then reaches out a hand, helping him.

REAL BOY   Who are you?

JAIME   Who am I? I am a part of you. I am your fears, I am the part you've closed the door to. I am your conscience.

REAL BOY   I don't know who you are!

REAL BOY drops to the floor.

REAL BOY   Please, just leave me be. I will be okay, here in this broken world full of twisted reflections and optical illusions of friendliness and good will...

JAMIE   Whose eyes are you seeing through? Am I truly scary, or were you told I was?

JAIME touches REAL BOY's forehead. Lights flash and then it's suddenly dark.

Soft lights pools on REAL BOY.

The soft light expands, and we see YOUNG REAL BOY and JAIME sat beside each other on chairs. This is a memory of a waiting room.

JAIME   Do you remember meeting me?

YOUNG BOY   What are you here for? You look normal.

YOUNG REAL BOY doesn't see REAL BOY. JAIME turns to answer YOUNG REAL BOY.

JAIME   You look normal too. I'm here because something is wrong.

YOUNG BOY   Nothing is ever wrong with girls who look like you.

JAIME   I hope the doctor is nice. Nice people always make uncomfortable situations easier.

YOUNG BOY   You're uncomfortable?

JAIME   Aren't you?

YOUNG BOY   Of course. No one wants to talk to these people. Are you here for bulimia? My older cousin had that. It's when you don't keep it in. Nobody noticed for a long time. But she's better now. She's like you.

JAIME   I don't have that. What do you mean like me?

YOUNG BOY   She's...shiny.

JAIME   You're shiny too.

JAIME points to something reflective on YOUNG REAL BOY, light up shoes or a metal wristwatch.

YOUNG BOY   Not like you and my cousin.

JAIME   Do you want to be?

YOUNG BOY   You never answered my question. What are you here for? Anxiety? Depression? My cousin told me about those too.

JAIME   I have a lot of reasons to be here. Just like you.

YOUNG BOY   I get night terrors. That's why I'm here.

MOTHER enters. She moves her mouth, calling to YOUNG REAL BOY but no sound comes out.

YOUNG BOY   You seem familiar somehow. Have we met before?

JAIME   Really? We haven't not met. But this is probably the first time you are open to truly seeing me. You tend to block me out.

JAIME is always invisible to MOTHER.

JAIME exits.

MOTHER   Where did you go in your head? I asked you something. Do you want me to go get you something from the vending machine? It will be a while until your turn.

YOUNG BOY   Thanks, Mama.

MOTHER   Of course, baby girl.

MOTHER is affectionate, hugging him before exiting. YOUNG REAL BOY turns back to the now empty chair.

YOUNG BOY   Weird girl.

Lights strobe in reverse to before and then dark. The sound of REAL BOY sobbing alone.

JAIME   You've been pushing me away since you started working with Dr. Oldrick.

JAIME leaves. TRUMAN enters.

TRUMAN   Come on, man. Where did you go?

TRUMAN finds REAL BOY, unconscious and curled up on the floor. He shakes REAL BOY. REAL BOY doesn't respond.

TRUMAN pulls out REAL BOY's phone.

TRUMAN   Figaro, hi, it's me - Truman. I need your help. We don't have the time for this. Shut up and listen! He's hurt. We are heading to the hospital. Could you contact his mother? I don't have the time to explain. Yes, we will meet there. Bye.

Lights flash red and blue, an ambulance.

Blackout.

Scene 22

TRUMAN paces. FIGARO enters, sees TRUMAN, explodes in anger.

FIGARO   What happened? What did you do to him? I knew you were bad news from the beginning!

FIGARO grabs TRUMAN. There's a scuffle as FIGARO starts a physical fight, TRUMAN responding: each getting a hit in. MOTHER enters. She pulls them apart.

MOTHER   You stop this right now! What's happened?

Long silence.

MOTHER   One of you start talking and give me answers. I deserve them.

FIGARO   Talk to Truman: he's the new best friend who clearly has dragged her down to his level. Has her taking drugs apparently.

TRUMAN   I...I found him...I never...I'm sorry.

MOTHER   When did you find her like this?

Silence.

MOTHER   ANSWER ME, TRUMAN! I am her mother, I deserve to know what has happened to my little girl okay?

TRUMAN   In the park, when I found him. He was hallucinating, fighting me... I've never seen him in a state like this.

MOTHER   What?

TRUMAN   He was fighting me.

MOTHER   Why are you calling my daughter that?

TRUMAN   He told me he's out to you –

MOTHER   None of my daughter's friends support that ridiculousness. So you've gotten her into drugs and you indulge this.

TRUMAN   I-? He prefers he/him pronouns. I only try to respect that –

MOTHER	Don't you dare! Who are you to teach me? I don't want to see you around my kid anymore. Ever again! You understand me? LEAVE!
TRUMAN	I was only -
MOTHER	Understand something, Truman. Boys like you are why mothers like me can't sleep at night. You ruin our daughters. The children that we spent years trying to raise. I love her. To save her from you I'm certain now. The only choice is to completely cut her off from boys like you. You'll no longer have access to my daughter. Cherish the time you had.
TRUMAN	What do you mean?
MOTHER	She's going to an all-girls boarding school as soon as she gets better. You won't be able to get to her there.
TRUMAN	Please. Don't.
MOTHER	I will not sacrifice my daughter's health for your happiness.

TRUMAN   I'll never talk to him again. I promise. But please don't do that to him. He'll be miserable.

MOTHER   No, you will. No more access to your little puppet. Other girls will do her good.

TRUMAN   No. Think how many schools he's moved from. This is the only one in which he isn't being bullied anymore. Will you move him to start the whole process again?

MOTHER   I will do what's best for my daughter.

TRUMAN   I love your 'daughter.' As a friend. So please, for her sake. Don't move her. You know I'm right. I will leave her alone for her happiness. Please.

Long pause.

MOTHER   Ok. (Beat.) You've made a good point. Start now. Leave. I don't want me or my daughter to ever have to hear your words again.

TRUMAN exits.

MOTHER   And you. Thank God for you Figaro.

Scene 23

REAL BOY is in a hospital bed.

MOTHER   I don't blame you darling. I don't. You're going to be ok. I am going to make sure you're ok.

REAL BOY   I'm sorry, Mama.

MOTHER   Shhhhh. Just rest. Focus on getting better. That's all I want from you now. Oh. My baby. My sweet baby. Shhhhhh. Shhhhhhhhhhhhhh.

REAL BOY   Mama I-.I Didn't ever mean for it to-

MOTHER   I know darling. I know. You're Mama's sweet girl. You're my good girl. It wasn't you. Figaro told me everything. I've already talked to that boy.

REAL BOY   Truman?

MOTHER   Yes, Truman. The boy who gave you those drugs.

REAL BOY   He brought me to the hospital. He didn't-

MOTHER   After giving you the poison. That is the important part.

REAL BOY   He didn't. I just smoked a cigarette that someone else-.

MOTHER   Truman probably laced it. How would you know? You've never smoked before.

REAL BOY   I-

MOTHER   No. You can't know. He took advantage of your innocence.

REAL BOY   I do know. He would never. Someone else-

MOTHER   I won't argue with you. You're sick. How quickly you've forgotten about Figaro. The one who is here in the hospital waiting to hear about you. The one who called me. The one who didn't put you on drugs.

REAL BOY   Of course I love Figaro. But he doesn't see me like Truman does.

MOTHER   Good. As he should.

REAL BOY   Mama, please. Leave it alone.

MOTHER   Ok. Rest. Enough talking about this. Just rest. Take your pills, darling. I don't like seeing you in pain.

REAL BOY   Thank you.

MOTHER   I'll go get more once you fall asleep.

Scene 24

Home. FIGARO and REAL BOY sit. They watch TV.

FIGARO How did the interview go?

REAL BOY It went really well honestly. Kinda surprised me that I did so well. Truman said he thought they held some type of prejudice against him. Asking him questions about if he could properly express sympathy for the clients.

FIGARO You're still hanging out with Truman? After what he did?

REAL BOY He didn't do anything. But, no. I think he's been really busy. Hasn't answered most of my texts. I was lucky I bumped into him there. He felt off though. Didn't want to look at me. As soon as I get better I'll try and meet him. See what's going on.

FIGARO Yeah?

REAL BOY Yeah. Is that a problem for you?

FIGARO   No. (beat) I don't understand why you continue to talk to the guy who almost got you killed. But I guess it's none of my business.

REAL BOY   It's not and he didn't.

FIGARO   Except it is since you're my best friend and I would really like to not see you die. So why? Do you like him or something?

REAL BOY   Of course I like him.

FIGARO   Oh, wow. So is it the sex? Is that why you can't let him go?

REAL BOY   Oh, ew! I'm not into him like that.

FIGARO   Oh.

REAL BOY   I'm straight.

FIGARO   I know that.

REAL BOY   So I'm not into guys like that. At all.

FIGARO   Oh.

REAL BOY   Yeah. That's cleared up?

FIGARO   Yes.

Long pause.

REAL BOY   Good. So, as I was saying I didn't really have the same problem as Truman. They just kinda wanted to know what my previous experience was and then we chit-chatted. The lady was actually really nice.

FIGARO   That's good. (beat) So you think you'll get the job?

REAL BOY   I do. I really do. I really need it. Mama's been horrible about giving me any money since-

FIGARO   I know.

REAL BOY   It's nice to be seen. The lady said I had a very nurturing spirit. I hope yours goes easy too.

FIGARO   I doubt it will.

REAL BOY   You don't know that.

FIGARO   It won't.

REAL BOY   You're kind. She'll see that and give you the job.

FIGARO   Kind isn't nurturing.

REAL BOY   Ok. But I think you're nurturing.

FIGARO   It's fine. Drop it.

REAL BOY   Ok. *(beat)* But you are! It's one of the best things about you.

FIGARO   You know nurturing is a code for woman right? Women. Are. Nurturing.

REAL BOY   That's not what she –

FIGARO   It is. You're trans but everyone can tell. She's fine calling you a boy but she's only giving you the job because she knows women do it best.

REAL BOY   I... So, when you ask me to... Do you
              even believe I'm –

FIGARO   – I call you a boy, don't I? What do you
              think?

REAL BOY   My biggest fear is that everyone is just
              lying to support my own madness.

FIGARO looks away.

FIGARO   Why do you always ask so much of the
              people around you?

REAL BOY   I don't know. The definition of insanity
              is doing the same thing and expecting
              different results. Not-asking is insanity,
              asking is insanity. My existence must
              be the physical embodiment of
              insanity.

FIGARO   Remember the spy games we used to
              love as children? We played pretend
              for years. Believing we were assassins,
              ninjas, double agents. We created fake
              stealth missions wherever we went.
              Sometimes we played against each
              other. Rivals hoping to prove our ninja

group was better than the other. That game never lasted long. We always found ourselves on the same side again. Could play for hours. Just us in our pretend world. And our world went everywhere with us. In Greece, with the mission of sneaking around without being noticed by any adults? Back then...we created our own secret non-verbal language...it felt amazing. Back then I was certain we are connected, we are meant to be together. But ever since...you started changing, wanting blue instead of pink...crying for my guns and throwing the doll my mom gave you for your birthday...it was like you started breaking that connection, slowly. Our telepathic language died. You changed. I mean we both did...I thought in the normal way, me becoming a man that loves to protect and you... a special someone I could protect. But instead...you turned out to be a real double agent. Not on my side, though. I am tired of being invisible for you. You betray me, your mom and any normal future for yourself, you betray

the life we could have had together...
You -!

They stare. FIGARO makes to leave.

FIGARO   Goodbye Mama. I'll see you when I see you.

FIGARO exits.

MOTHER   Bye! Where is Figaro going? I thought he was staying for dinner.

REAL BOY He's not.

MOTHER   Oh. Is something wrong?

REAL BOY No. He just had to go.

MOTHER   Well he has better manners than that. And "I'll see you when I see you". As if the boy won't be here tomorrow or the day after.

REAL BOY He won't. So you can just stop.

MOTHER   What do you mean he won't?

REAL BOY   I mean I'm not seeing Figaro anymore. He's not coming back to this house. We aren't friends.

MOTHER   Ok. Well this isn't the first time you and him have gotten into it and this won't be the last.

REAL BOY   No, Mama. This time is real. He said something that can't be- It can't be taken back or fixed, or looked past or looked over, or changed, or misconstrued in any other way but what he meant.

MOTHER   What did he say?

REAL BOY   He-! You wouldn't understand.

MOTHER   Well if I wouldn't understand, clearly it's not that bad.

REAL BOY   You're just going to take his side anyway so there's no point in discussing it with you. He's not coming back. He doesn't want to and neither do I. That's it.

MOTHER You are throwing away your only true friendship. For what? For what? I don't understand you child. I've never pretended to. But I thought I understood the simple things about you. The basic things. We all need friendship. We all need care. He gives you that. He's stayed with you through- all of this-. And now over one fight about something you can not talk about you are willing to let it all go. To run to who? Huh? The drug boy? The one who almost got you killed? Where did the smart young lady I raised go? Where did the one who listened to their Mama and did everything in their power to be kind to others, to be understanding, where did she go? I want her back. Please. I want the daughter who bent over backwards to help people, who forgave easily and wasn't always so angry. Why are you always so angry? Your anger will eat you all up. I see it. It's pushing away the people you care about. Figaro cares about you.

REAL BOY   No, he doesn't. Not in the way he is supposed to.

MOTHER   You can not ask people to only love you in the exact way you want to be loved. That is not fair.

REAL BOY   You're right. But don't I have the right to reject the love that hurts me because of the way they choose to give it?

MOTHER   Lonely. You'll be lonely one day. Keep down this path. Heaven help me. I know you no longer listen to me but if you listen to anything please take this - Stop making yourself so difficult to love. I'll always fight to love you, but others will not. You've just thrown away the closest thing to a forever type of love. He loves you. He may one day want to marry you. That is your future that's just walked out the door. Please!

Scene 25

REAL BOY tries to greet TRUMAN at the park. There's nothing special in the sky, this time. TRUMAN pulls back. REAL BOY's hand freezes in mid-air. It's awkward.

TRUMAN So, what is it? Why did you call me to meet up?

REAL BOY Well, I wanted to talk...to apologize. I know my mom was probably rude to you at the hospital. I also wanted to catch up with you, you know. You didn't seem ok at the interview. We are friends, right? If you are going through something you can tell me.

TRUMAN We had a deal. We were partners brought together by a deal. You teach me to study, I teach you to be a man. Nothing more. Nothing less.

REAL BOY But-- Did someone tell you to say this? Talk to me!

TRUMAN This- we are over, okay? I don't care and I never did. I got my marks. Thanks

>for that. I've fulfilled my part of the deal. You don't need me anymore. You fought off your bullies. You've stepped into what you want the world to see. You're a real boy.

Pause.

TRUMAN   At least as much as you can be. It was a fantasy, that I don't want to be a part of anymore, okay? I don't owe you my time anymore and neither do you. Just go back to your fancy, quiet, little life and leave me be.

REAL BOY slowly nods. TRUMAN exits. REAL BOY pulls out the pill bottle. He swallows what he can. Moment of silence. Then his body starts convulsing. REAL BOY then lays still.

Scene 26

REAL BOY is spinning. From different angles spawn horrible, swirling figures: MOTHER, FIGARO, DR.OLDRIK, HEAD BULLY. They circle REAL BOY.

MOTHER I want my lovely girl back. Where has she gone, huh? You are not my child anymore.

FIGARO Won't you go on a date with me? Come on, deep down you know we're great together! Mama thinks so too! Just make us happy!

DR. OLDRIK You can't do that, you are a sweet little girl, behave like one if you want to be happy!

TRUMAN You know I'm not REALLY your friend, right?

REAL BOY drops on the floor. Everything gets louder.

HEAD BULLY Why you crying like a girl, huh? You sissy!

REAL BOY screams out.

JAIME enters, tries to reach him, save him from the hurt. REAL BOY runs. JAIME chases. He spins, falls to the ground in exhaustion. JAIME bends down over him.

JAIME   Boy, wake up! Get back to yourself. Look around you! How long can you keep mirroring, splitting your personality in tiny bits of reflections of what the world tells you to be? Come on, please, let me back in! You've stopped hearing me again!

REAL BOY doesn't reply, just holds his head and cries. JAIME slaps him. He jumps finally responds.

REAL BOY   SHUT UP! Why do you keep appearing in these different forms? I DON'T WANT YOU AROUND ME! I AM FINE. I AM FINE. I CAN BE FINE.

JAIME   YOU ARE NOT FINE!

Silence.

JAIME   Punching and kicking is not the only thing that makes you a boy. Hanging out with the people that hurt you, won't make you more loved. Why do you only go to the extremes? Either completely denying who you are or becoming a toxic version of it.

REAL BOY   So, have you come to gloat about my inevitable downfall?

JAMIE   I never gloat.

REAL BOY   What? You're right so much you never need to gloat?

JAMIE   I care so much I don't gloat. I am not the enemy here. I am here to help.

REAL BOY   Here to help. How have you helped so far? Have you stopped me from being sent here? Have you convinced Mama of my sanity? Have you helped me keep any of my friendships? Or have you just been there every step of the way to see my failure and watch it all burn?

JAIME   I have been there, yes. I have tried to help you. But I am not exactly you. I

                    can not force you to listen to what I
                    have to say.

REAL BOY   What do you say? You say the same
                    nothing over and over again.

JAIME   I repeat the words that validate your
                    existence. Because they are true.

REAL BOY   You are not true.

JAIME   I am not real. But I am true. I am
                    truthful with you. You aren't rejecting
                    me. You're rejecting the truth in favor
                    of a temporary happiness provided by
                    the people who will not accept the
                    real you. I accept you. I always have. I
                    am the part of you that is not you.

REAL BOY   Temporary happiness. You are
                    temporary. You don't know anything.
                    You don't know what it's like. You can't
                    possibly know what my life is like.

JAIME   You live a life for everyone else.

REAL BOY   I live a life to live.

JAIME   You're not really living.

REAL BOY   What is this then? I just happen to be pushing air in and out of my lungs and pumping blood?

JAIME   You're being a scared little child in a hidey little hole, just breathing, just pumping blood and doing nothing more! You're going to let your fear and your wants slowly dry you out until you die into a drug induced husk. Stop feeling sorry for yourself. Get up and do something.

REAL BOY   I am.

JAIME   This isn't something. This is a pitiful attempt at holding onto things you shouldn't hold on to.

REAL BOY   Those things can include you.

REAL BOY subdues JAIME. It's a violent smothering.

Scene 27

It's bright, it's uncomfortable.

REAL BOY   Mama-

MOTHER   Baby. You know I love you. And I wish I could help you. But I can't.

REAL BOY   You can. Just help me.

MOTHER   I don't know what you need baby.

REAL BOY   I need… I need…

MOTHER   I'm here.

REAL BOY   Love me, please.

MOTHER   I do.

REAL BOY   Do you love a son?

MOTHER   I love my child.

REAL BOY   Love me, please.

MOTHER	My child has a drug problem. You have a drug problem. So I'm going to get you somewhere they can fix it. Because I love you. Unselfishly, and unconditionally. This is love.
REAL BOY	Don't lock me away in a box. Please. I know I'm not easy. But don't hide me, put me away.
MOTHER	I know this is the drugs talking.
REAL BOY	Mama all I've wanted-
MOTHER	Baby, the world is hard enough. Why must you make your life harder? Why can't you realize?
REAL BOY	I don't want to be this way.
MOTHER	I know. Mama will fix it, baby. My love for you is unconditional.
REAL BOY	How will you fix it, Mama? Mama, can you look at me? Mama, can you look at me? Mama why can't you look at me, Mama?

MOTHER   I won't be here forever.

REAL BOY   You're a bad mother.

MOTHER   You don't mean that. You're just on the drugs.

REAL BOY   You don't love me.

MOTHER   You're loved. You're so loved. I love you. I want what's best for you. I know you can't see that.

REAL BOY   I can never see anything. All these voices, pulling me apart.

MOTHER   We'll talk when you get out.

REAL BOY   We may not.

MOTHER   We will.

REAL BOY   Oh mother.

REAL BOY walks, half-dragged, accompanied by masked nurses into the mental health facility. MOTHER yells after him.

MOTHER   We will. I love you. I love you. I love you.

Scene 28

REAL BOY sits upright. There's that uncomfortable music again, from when REAL BOY usually speaks with JAIME, but now it's in the background. REAL BOY's legs are tied to the bed. His movements are slow and controlled, mechanical. Like a puppet.

NURSE   Time for your pills, darling. Ah, ah you know the magic rules, darling. If you want it to work, you have to repeat it. Repeat it. 'I am a girl'. I am a girl.

Light fades out steadily, then back on! A stunningly bright spotlight shines on a wooden, Pinocchio doll.

Then the light fades fast.

Scene 29

Abruptly cheerful music. FIGARO stands in a tux. MOTHER in a nice dress. It's clearly a special day.

MOTHER   I always knew you two would work it out. I always did. Oh, Figaro. My son.

They hug.

MOTHER   Now go. She can't see you.

FIGARO exits.

MOTHER   Darling! Come here! He's gone.

REAL BOY enters. He's more feminine in presentation than we've ever seen. He's clearly uncomfortable but pushing through it, for MOTHER.

MOTHER   I'm so proud of you. This is the day that every mother dreams of for her child. That you'll one day dream of for yours. When I held you when you were first born, I spoke all these wonderful dreams over you. That you would be smart, and loving, and kind, and find a nice man who wanted to give you the world. Now that's all happening and yet I'm crying. I don't want to let you go.

REAL BOY You don't have to, Mama.

MOTHER I know. I know.

MOTHER signals for REAL BOY to turn. She spritzes him with perfume. He's learnt how to not react.

MOTHER I love you.

REAL BOY I love you too Mama.

MOTHER exits and quickly returns with a big bagged white wedding dress. She hangs it up prominently, unzips the dress bag to reveal it. Then walks off. REAL BOY stares at it. Then he stares out at the audience.

THE END

www.ingramcontent.com/pod-product-compliance
Lightning Source LLC
Chambersburg PA
CBHW042117100526
44587CB00025B/4093